In B

Daniel Hood

In Brine

Daniel Hood

I would like to dedicate this to anyone who's ever lent me a cig.

Contents:

A Festive Saga

I knew he was in the room before I'd even opened my eyes. I sat up in my bed and saw him stood at the foot of my bed. I knew who he was and I knew he knew exactly who I was. He looked like I'd always imagined he would have. Stood there in my apartment at 2 AM. The entire world in a deep, black sleep but for us. Locking eyes.
My room got longer. I was no longer in bed but in a large room. An impossibly large room that seemed to go on forever in each direction. We were on a metal walkway with barriers at each side to avoid toppling into the perpetual abyss. All around there was multitude of complex steam powered machinery and whirring cogs. The rusted contraptions seemed ancient but appeared to run perfectly. The noise of the constant chugging of the Titanic wheels began feel overwhelmingly oppressive to the point where I began screaming for it to end.

The man put his hand on my shoulder and said "Be calm." and I was. He was as old as time with his listless tired eyes, long neglected white beard and tattered red coat. He walked with a hunched back and a limp down the walkway. I followed behind but in spite of his apparent enfeeblement I couldn't seem to catch up to him. I broke into a jog and eventually a sprint, always the old man was just out of reach.

Suddenly I wasn't on a walkway surrounded by machinery anymore but in a what seemed to be a workshop. There were lots of tiny work stations all around. At these stations there were unusual creatures of about a foot high. They were nude, sexless creatures with dull grey skin, pointed ears and beady black eyes. I then noticed that, while they had mouths, they had all been crudely stitched shut, dried blood still noticeable, if only just. At their work surfaces there were small piles of wood, nails and screws along with paint, glue and other craft equipment. They were using their tiny hands to produce things such as toy trains and other basic children's playthings at astonishing speeds, never once faltering or slowing down. "What are these?" I asked The Man. "The help." he responded. "Who's help?" I asked. He simply shook his head and turned away. We were no longer in the workshop but outside. All around was snow and nothing more. I was lost in an ocean of white with this strange man. Then an awful high pitched whistling noise began. It was the man. He was calling for something. He looked up at the sky and I looked with him. Suddenly something was falling down towards us. I could make out the shape of a sledge, just like I'd always known. It was being pulled by reindeer. Of course it was. It gracefully landed in front of us. The animals what seemed to be reindeer appeared to be normal save for the fact that they had no eyes and just like the grey creatures of the workshop had their mouths stitched shut. The man stepped onboard the sledge. "Join me" he said. I did. We were up in the air. He knew where to go. I knew he knew. We were in a house, many houses, all at once. I was watching him. He was giving gifts, gifts of happiness, luck, joy. Not trinkets like I heard in the story. He also gave suffering, loss and tragedy. Unspeakable anguish. Little Boys found not breathing on their Christmas morning by their parents. "Do you understand?" he asked? I did.

"You try." and I did. He watched. I gave and I took to one and all. We would go back to the workshop sometimes. I would get more to give from the tiny grey men and get back on the sledge and see people. I watched children grow. I watched people grow old. Families get smaller. Families appear. Go back to the grey men. Give. Take. The man had stopped watching me by now. I kept on. Giving. Taking. Giving. Taking. My beard had grown long. I was tired. It was time to stop. I choose a house. I choose my successor. I was in his room. He knew I was in the room before He'd even opened his eyes.

In Brine

Help . I'm stuck. The air is thick. It makes me feel
sick. Sick in mind and tired body but nothing hits
the soul. That revered and sacred spark is gone.
It's a daunting endless hole
A well, a pit, a council bin of festering shit.
Is salvation running late? I cannot tell time. Allow
me to self medicate. Booze fags and seething hate.
I'm a cunt preserved in brine.
The friend left behind. The spectre with no feast.
The rest went to el dorado where the streets are
paved with gold. I'm locked up in the attic turning
into mould. I leave behind no heirs and let's not
speak of grace. There will be no changing of the
guard. The national guard shall have the head of
this international disgrace.

The Unfortunate Eruption

The thing about committing suicide, it isn't always about not being sad enough to actually go through with the act, lord knows if that's all it took them there'd be a hell of a lot less of us, neither indeed is it about being too scared, be it of pain or what lies in the great beyond. It's mainly down to all the bloody effort of preparation. Matthew had decided to kill himself around last Christmas and give himself a year's prep time, after roughly seven years of simmering self loathing and dissatisfaction with his spineless and submissive nature. Matthew was a short, bespectacled, chubby little man, not exactly easy on the eye but that didn't really matter as no one ever bothered looking at him anyway. He worked in retail, the same store for the past 12 years as it happens. Never excelling beyond his entry level job. Not due to any ineptitude on his part, but because the higher ups never took any notice of him and he never had to guts to ask for such a promotion. Matthew had taken solace, for years in his hobby of homemade machines and contraptions, he'd often be tinkering way into the night with various gadgets, his beady eyes peering through the thick lenses of his glasses at his fingers masterfully altering and modifying the tiny machines in toy cars and talking teddy bears. His modest one bedroom house was adorned with all sorts of wonderfully inventive contraptions. Walking dinner trays, automatic tea making machines, talking toasters. His most prized invention was his amazing tinsel blaster. It was practically the only thing that made anyone take any notice of him. It was strapped to his torso and funnels which went down his arms connected to the tinsel storage unit, the tinsel was fired out of the funnels. All this was hidden underneath his Christmas jumper, giving the appearance of tinsel shooting out of his hands. "Amazing" is how he felt about this when he first conceived it. When he unveiled it in the staff room three Christmases ago, he was overjoyed with the stunned silence from his colleagues, which was in actuality an indifferent silence. He had however, decided that since it got such a positive reaction he would endeavour to present this to his work colleagues every Christmas, just to make working the holidays that much easier. As I stated earlier though, his hobby had however, failed the abate the crushing self loathing this unfortunate little man had endured. In his one year plan to top himself, he'd been looking into building a very clever little contraption. A bomb. Something that was timed to go off in his home so he could go out in a blaze of glory surrounded by his creations. To leave with dignity. That's all a man can ask surely? He planned to work his Christmas shift, amaze everyone with his tinsel display, go home, sit down with a discount brandy and shuffle off this mortal coil. Matthew looked at the clock. 8:45. He was nearly late for work so he frantically grabbed his tinsel machine and bolted out the door. It was oddly cathartic working what he knew would be his final shift ever in a store he had become so used to. Never again would he see Desmond pushing the trolleys in the car park or Mary who works in frozen goods with her nipples perking up when she reached into the freezer to get a Chicago town pizza. His moment was almost up. It was lunch. He pottered into the staff room. This is the last time he would ever make a difference. He marched into where everyone was tucking into a poorly prepared government regulation turkey, spread his legs apart to add effect and shouted "It's the Christmas display!" His voice cracked due to emotion and nerves. He pressed the button at his back to start the tinsel show and raised his hands out. Nothing. Matthew wasn't sure what was wrong. He stood there awkwardly. Then he started beeping. He knew what was wrong. His heart dropped. "Fiddlesticks!" he squealed and scarpered out if the staff room. The staff just went back to their turkey dinner. "Weird little cunt" someone said. Matthew was in the bathroom in one of the stalls. In his haste to get to work on time he'd accidently strapped his homemade bomb to his torso instead of his tinsel machine! He had to get it off and deactivate it! He was having a hard time getting his Christmas jumper off. He could get one arm out. Yes well played. Other arm now. He struggled with that one. Eventually he got it out, now just to get his head out. a lot harder this time. Struggling. Tries to pull it off. the beeping is getting faster. His heads finally freed. Now to..oh, too late.

The explosion did kill him as he had planned, so in one way it was a success, however in the struggle to get his jumper off, he had replaced the bomb on his torso, inadvertently putting it out his lower back, blowing his arse off in the bog. His death was ruled to have been caused by explosive diarrhoea brought on by bad minced pies.

His death was reported in page 12 of his local rag. 'RESIDENT OAF DIES IN VIOLENT ANUS ERRUPTION.'

He will be remembered.

Cloudy Peaks

Well she lived over an hour away, next to the pad of an old serial killer and she used to launch throwing knives at an old mattress in her front yard and she used to paint penises on oil canvases and kept them in the living room and she refused to ever own a TV and she owned an axe but refused to say way and she kept her old wedding dress that had seen better days and she rode a bike in the nude and she once sold cocaine to Mark E Smith and she knew everything about trees and when she got drunk she sang old opera standards and she could lift impossibly heavy metal bars with ease and she walked five miles to work over cloudy peaks every morning. I once came over and she was holding a baby. "Who's is that?" "Fucked if I know you dickhead and she cut it off because she said I was too strange

Rum & Wine

Your day begins around three or four. You open your eyes and rise from your bedroom floor. Well now you're over 6ft tall but not a giant anymore. Those days are past. It's your crumpled back. It's your sullen eyes. Red from booze and 4am when the little boy inside you cries. "This life isn't mine let's try again" but squalors where you've made your den. You stagger outside with a walk like mine. Will it be beer, rum or wine. Anything to kill the time. Another 26 years or however old I am, until you're back on your feet and we'll meet. A mirror image, but until then you're just a mirage as you're guzzling full's and halves. Until then I can't get mad, after all you are my dad.

In Frost

It's cold. The frost is coming on. My arms are frozen. I can't feel my legs. I can feel my skin and hair constrict as the cruel cracking and snapping grip of ice smoothers me. It's cold but I don't feel cold. I fee nothing now. As cold as it is now, I am conscious of a flicker. An embryo of flame. An unborn torrent of heat. If I could only move my fucking legs. The small ember inside, is it the death rattled of a man or is it the sun so far away? A huge star in the horizon. Past the black. A sun that shines like I've heard so much. Past the choking ices grip is the embrace, the love, the peace. That's where I need to be. That's where I will be. It's cold but it's not a life sentence. Not if there's any justice. I'll make a promise to feel that comfort. The sun will caress my skin and I'll be free. It's there now. It's blazing orange haze. Miles away from here. I could move my fucking legs I could walk towards it. I could be in the green grass of a new land and I'd hope you'd hold my hand as we walk through it. The sun smiling down on us. It's cold right now but when I can move my fucking legs I'll be in that road. I'll see you there. You'll see me. I'll be bathed in light.

Wake Up

It's 5:45am. Eagerly awaiting their father son fishing trip, Martin, Andrews dad, was sat there at the kitchen table that morning in his fishing gear, but all any observer would probably notice is his baby puke green bucket hat, adorned with a variety of little fishing hooks which, in spite of giving him immense pride of purchase, you really couldn't deny that he looked like a bit of a tit. Even if he was aware of what a clueless peanut headed man he looked, the grin could not be removed from his rubbery slab of face. Martin and Andrew had planned this over a year ago. They had fastidiously researched B&B's around the east coast of the UK and purchased some of the best fishing equipment on the market. The excitement in that kitchen could be cut with a knife. Popping down to get something from the fridge, Samantha, the half awake wife of Martin and mother of Andrew stood there looking quizzically through almost open eyes at her goof of a spouse sat at the table.

"What are you doing up in that gear Martin?"

"Fishing trip today love." You're still going? Who with?" "Me and the lad obviously." Samantha's pressed her hands to her forehead, trying to process things at this early hour of the morning. "Martin, I thought we'd talked about this." "We did but I think it's best the boy got out for the day. Fresh air in the lungs and ocean breezes. He'll soon come round!" "Please give it some thought. Neither of you will enjoy it." Martin didn't give it some thought because he wasn't the thinking type really and began tying up his hefty walking boots and whistling a jaunty tune, accompanied by the backing tune of Samantha groaning "for fucks sake" as she stormed out of the kitchen.

Nothing could dampen Martins chipper spirits, not even the fact that since planning this glorious expedition 12 months ago, Andrew had turned 13, and in accordance with cosmic law that all adolescence must adhere to, he became an obstinate little shit. He's in his room all the time doing god knows what, going away for days on end and coming back looking like he's not had a good solid meal. A lot of people would've given up had they been in Martins position. But not Martin. If anything this strengthened his resolve.

It came the time for tracks to be made, Andrew was still in his bed asleep and it was almost 8:00! No matter. Martin was a persuasive sort and there's nothing to but a spring back into a boys step like some enthusiastic patter from his father. He marched his way up the stairs, obliviously knocking over a plant plot with his backpack and treading on the cat as he lumbered his way up into his sons room.

"Rise and shine Andy old chap" he bellowed as he opened the curtains to reveal a tedious grey sky. "Beautiful day for it. You know what today is don't you?" Andrew groaned from underneath the sheets. "It's our fishing trip son!" said Martin as he plonked himself on the bed in an attempt to rouse his son. "Remember we're meant to be setting off today. The glorious east coast. Grimsby! Remember we were gonna go see where Craig Riley lived and get a picture of Grimsby Dock Tower. Are you excited?" Andrew again groaned.

"Dad pleeeease." he said. "You say please dad now but you'll be thank your dad later on when you're guzzling on a Solero on the way back with our Simply Red mix tape on in the car."

"Ere have a look at this." Martin reached into his bag and produced a Tupperware box full of worms. "Real bait. We could get us some proper fish with this Andy!" Martin opened the box and put it close to his sons face. Any was pale. "Proper expensive gear too. Look at this fishing rod. Best on the market." Andrew was uninterested. "Set us back a few quid but that's the price you pay for quality. Look at the sheen on that shaft!"Martin began haphazardly and enthusiastically swinging his expensive fishing rod around his sons room. "Look at the smooth action on that! Ooh shit!" Martin in his misguided keenness had accidentally smashed his son's bedroom window open. "Oh no. Erm I might be able to fix this." He turned around quickly to face the damage and again causing a calamity in the form of catching his fishing rod on the clear plastic tube by Andrews bed. Just at that moment Samantha came into the room "What on earth was that noise? Oh my god Andrew! Martin what have you done? He's not well Martin. You know he's not well and you're making it worse!"

"I'm sorry Sammy..he's not all that bad. Bit of fresh air. Bit of fresh air'll do him good..."

They never did bother going fishing in the end. There wasn't really much point. Martin did stand by his words though. All Andrew needed was a good day out and some wind in his hair. He didn't give up his relentless chiming though. Every morning. "Come on Andy. Spot of football while it's nice out?" It was never any use. "I've got you that Sonic collection for your Xbox. It's two player!" It was all pointless. Months tumbled along as they do and Martins still there. "Aye up lazy bones. Any news? We've just been to town your mother and I and I was looking in HMV and I saw they had that Lego Batman film on DVD. Your mum said not to bother but I've got it for you anyway. Treacle tart for afters today n all so I'll see you at the table for that one no doubt. I'll remember to record Family Guy for you as well if I can work that bloody machine, which reminds me you still need to show me how to work. Anyway I think your mothers calling me."

Martin leaves the gravestone and walks back to car.

"He'll be fine. Just needs some fresh air"

These Eyes

If only my eyes were hers, if only she could see with these eyes of mine. If only she could see the way she looks at mine. If only she could feel the soft skin against mine. If only she could visit the fortress of herself and take stock of what I've found. Beneath the coal she's dug up I've found diamonds to wear in her crown. She'll glimmer in the midday sun. Just like those eyes that look back into mine

God of Heck Fire

It's a 10,000 degree dead heat between women wine and cocaine. The songs in retirement engulfed by the flame. There's a cinder in his wake and a parade as he walks. There's a devil on his shoulder but that fuckers all talk. A privilege to behold and a danger to witness. We cannot take your heat so we walk behind and gasp and cheer and cry and laugh and put our hands firmly on your shoulder and tell you how much we value you.

Tourist Information

It's the same old story. Well chew me up and spit me out you monstrous pig. I'm caught in the belly of this defunct Dickensian wale and the innards are full of claw marks and bad graffiti. I'm wading towards the bar through a swamp of bad directions and mothers ruin. The jukebox is screaming and the walls are bleeding. We're all fluent in small talk around here and no one dare whisper over all the shouting. We've seen it all through the cracked window of this last chance saloon. As we lay here screaming in the soul, the old mill stands with a cold indifference. The old mills seen it all and cared for nothing.

The Squire (unfinished rumination)

I was saved by a devil. The angels ignored me after I stopped taking their calls. He came to me after about six beers in a blaze of glory wielding a sledgehammer. A figure of solid muscle and cold eyes. Hands that know the cartography of this dead valley. A frame contorted by alarming jolts of bad decisions and punishing circumstances. It takes a sight like that to jar your mind out of the quagmire of self pity and boozy fumes I find myself knee deep in more times than I care to mention. I thought I was long out of the game but its cards on the table. This was a dishonest man but honest about what he was. I would have judged him and rightly so, but as it goes I was saved by a devil and there's nothing more pathetic and naive than a man in need of salvation.

Mark E Smith Wouldn't Like This

Squirrels of Salford sleep tight tonight
Don't let the hedge clippers bite
your furry head shall feel no snip
and I'll always remember Mark E Smith

Lady of the sea

From years ago I wrote this about her Our lady of the sea

From the waif of my knee
Your immunity to night time
Never failed to impress me

In the dungeon of the mad
Underneath the bloody rag
You're there in a white rose
You're there in a clearing I no longer go
You slipped through my fingers and into blue sky
You took me for a ride over fields with the angel
you became with my rose tinted eye

I still study those parchments from a thousand
years and a thousand women ago
A thousand drinks to douse the flame I still carry
for you. A feeble flame I hope you don't
remember.
A different figure I hope you'll never know.

Sorry

I'd sworn you a view of trees of green and seas of blue
I'd promised you champagne and a smile every morning for breakfast
I never knew that promise was empty from an empty vessel
Behind the music there was just static
My satellite is out of range
I was meant to be the anchor to steady your ship in choppy seas
and we'd sit on the dock of the bay watching tides roll away
I was the anchor but I dragged you kicking and screaming into the briny deep
That same murky depths where you found I'd slept for a thousand years
I'm sorry, I could see you were drowning but I was so caught up in the seaweed down here I couldn't and wouldn't move to act.
You eventually broke free from my rusty chains
and now you'll sore to the surface and rise up onto the surface of a calm and beautiful morning

You'll see trees of green and seas of blue and drink
champagne

Step outside and kiss the world
You are marvellous and share it with the rest of
them
They could do with someone like you

I'm sorry.
All my love.
Daniel

Cancel My Dinner

It was to be a warm meal and a lot of time made up for. Father and son laughing and talking over yams, sweet potato, spiced jerk meat, rice and pea. At the end you'd say sorry and I know you'd meant it. But we've had to delay. You had an appointment booked with some special brew and a park bench instead of your not so special boy. I wonder if this was a warning. Would it be a dinner with an unwanted but expected guest of the black dog that's devoured you and begin a new meal of its own starting with my toes. A cancelled dinner has bought us closer in spirit than any number of unattended birthday parties. We are two souls falling into the same mine shaft. We shall not be excavated. We will be ignored for the diamonds. Doomed to the soil doomed to the dog. Damn that dog and we're as dammed as it is.

Canada 2009

I didn't know anything. I was 18 years old. Landing through unimportant circumstances at an important place in time. West of England and north of the USA. Canada in 2009. This ripe face with cheeky green eyed marvelling a skyline which surely inspired the descriptions of paradise from days of antiquity. These mountains. Surely something other than nature or man or any god could build such terrifying sights on this mere planet of which I'd seen so little of. These mountains demanding me to explain myself. Why such a small and stupid boy would dare behold them. To this very day as I write this I yearn to bear witness to them again. They were high peaks and we got higher still within their forests around the safety of the campfire with laughter and passing pipes and listening to so many Fleetwood Mac songs on low quality speakers which were to me an angels choir. This along with trying and failing to impress local nubiles disinterested in the feeble patter of this foolish boy in the one and only bar for sweeping miles was as important to my own adolescence as an audience with three pope is to a Roman Catholic. A magic was instilled on me. On the many acre farm. In that suburban house party. In those nine hour drives. In those desolate prairies. In that sunset I viewed from the balcony betwixt two peaks. There was a magic given to me that sometimes in those fleeting private moments, makes me 18 and stupid and smiling as the crystal lake glimmers and as the big bear roars and all of time stands still. I'm Canada 2009.

Notes

Printed in Great Britain
by Amazon